Visiting Ghosts and Ground

poems by

Stacy W. Dixon

Finishing Line Press
Georgetown, Kentucky

Visiting Ghosts and Ground

Copyright © 2018 by Stacy W. Dixon
ISBN 978-1-63534-459-2 First Edition
All rights reserved under International and Pan-American Copyright Conventions. No part of this book may be reproduced in any manner whatsoever without written permission from the publisher, except in the case of brief quotations embodied in critical articles and reviews.

ACKNOWLEDGMENTS

Grateful acknowledgment is made to the editors of the following publications in which these poems first appeared:

Encore: "Night Terror"
The Mid-America Poetry Review: "Sanguine," "Quiet Places"
Tiger's Eye: "The Question," "Kindred Incantations," "I'm Still Your Child," "Visiting Ghosts and Ground," "Annie's Men," "Shelf Life."
Pirene's Fountain: "Shedding Skin"
The Provo Orem Word Review: "From a Stolen Child"
Exponent II: "The Middle"
Sweet Tree Review: "Night Muse"
SAND and SKY: Poems from Utah: "Canyon Calling," "Mother of My Bones"

A few of these poems were published by Tiger's Eye Press (2010) in a chapbook titled *A Pebble Thrown in Water*.

Publisher: Leah Maines
Editor: Christen Kincaid
Cover Art: Marianne Goodell
Author Photo: Micah Julin
Cover Design: Elizabeth Maines McCleavy

Printed in the USA on acid-free paper.
Order online: www.finishinglinepress.com
also available on amazon.com

Author inquiries and mail orders:
Finishing Line Press
P. O. Box 1626
Georgetown, Kentucky 40324
U. S. A.

Table of Contents

Night Terror 1

Spider Memories.. 2

Sanguine 3

Quiet Places... 4

Shedding Skin 5

Mother of My Bones 6

Shelf Life 7

Jaded House of Moons... 8

Whale Watching 9

Night Muse 10

The Middle 11

Life in Reverse.. 12

Underneath 13

Visiting Ghosts and Ground 14

Kindred Incantations 16

Canyon Calling 17

Annie's Men... 18

A Love for Loneliness 19

Dreaming Herself Alive... 20

From a Stolen Child 21

The Question... 23

Still your Child.. 25

For Dakota, Carson, and Micah . . . always.

"In the midst of winter, I found there was, within me, an invincible summer."
—*Albert Camus*

Night Terror

No sleep for the one
who wants it.
No dream deep enough
to fall into.

No chasm dark enough
to hide from the ivy
which grows faster at night,
creeping up the house,
longing to get in the windows.

I stare into the black
until it becomes a snowstorm
of dancing dots,
a television with no picture,

imagine the flowers
in my garden
leaning over to rest,
folding in their loveliness
for another day.

The thought makes me drowsy,
but I stay awake.
I hear the rustling.
The ivy's got a foothold
on another brick.

Spider Memories

I can't call it enough adjectives
to plug the venom
it wants to inject me with.
The heaviest shoe within reach

is in my hand.
I'm balancing on a stepping stool,
which I dislike almost as much
as spiders.

Like the little silken
thread babies hatching
in kaleidoscope hundreds
down my bedroom wall.

The one that hung
above my mother's bed,
she yelled at me
because she was too weak,

so I stood on the bed,
purged its insides with a book.
Cursed the mess dead things
leave behind.

Almost as much as the way
I'm hesitating now,
to crush it
on this damn stool

that won't hold still.
Two crying voices behind me,
waiting for me
to finish it.

Sanguine

The night was thick,
black,
like deep water
in a dark building.
But the sky,
while she breathed,
sanguine.

A color to imprint
the back of my eyes,
sleep there.
A lasting dream
of my mother.

Spots on the floor,
I treasured like
stained glass ornaments,
fearing leaving,
she would take them.

Her journey was not cushioned
by an egg-crate mattress,
nor did my pleading
convince the sky
to give its color
back to her lips.

Quiet Places

A pebble thrown in water
and the ripples it creates,
reminders of a moment
once again.

*There's a place for him
in your heart,*
she said,
*where we put away
the past
and move on
to what is real.*

A memory
or two, at least.
Safe and hidden,
not to interfere with
houses and husbands
and sacred children.
Kept in silence,
never spoken,
a thought on embers lies.

A river runs so softly
over stones
that it has shaped,
ever faithful
to the way
the water flows.

Shedding Skin

I don't know, the doctor told her.
Laser treatments are painful,
there are so many.
And there would be scarring.
You should think about that.
But she didn't.
Wanted only to shimmy herself
between two cutting edges,
leaving the shell of tattooed skin
behind in one whole piece
like a snake.
Behind closed eyelids,
she remembered
how she once craved the pain
of her sewn on colors.
But that could go away
after the shedding.
Her body pink,
naked, and slippery.
Renewed as one born
of water.

Mother of my Bones

You have something
to do with this.
I feel it in my bones,
feel you in my bones.

You send pieces
of yourself to me.
In dreams,
or maybe
through an open window.

I feel it in my bones,
feel you in my bones.
Things from there,
you could not do here
with a broken body.

Shelf Life

Stay in heaven, dead boy.
Days once numbered
are renewed by the trees
you climbed.

The pony who turned back
to the corral when you rode him,
takes you over the mountain
past the sun.

Flesh returns to your bones
through the eyes of a black-haired girl,
there on the sofa
behind the fiction.

She brings you back
for hours every evening.
Maybe as you were,
or she would have you be.

Don't be deceived
by your lack of a body.
There's a light on
over your days,
when the doors are locked.

Stay in heaven, dead boy.
The rider has returned
to the Nightland
without you.

Jaded House of Moons

It is a house of giving,
a jaded house of moons
and moons.
Round with shine,
pregnant with promise.

Where I stay my place,
between pressed pages
of words kept silent.

Without the words,
I would drift away,
away down the halls
at night, in a dream

from a house of moons
and moons.

Whale Watching

On our whale watching trip
we picture ourselves
in the middle of the blue
on our globe.

While we use words to our children
like *vast* and *free*,
the crabs pull their own
back into the trap.

Night Muse

On a page, words only lie,
written hurriedly in the night,
fearing the idea
will run away and reveal itself
to another more fit
to arrange them.

The Middle

Watering your flowers today
at the cemetery

it was so quiet.
We decided to walk.

The kids picked up
cherry tree blossoms
to leave on graves

in the old section.
We read headstones of those
dead one hundred years.

We were there
on the path,

strangely together.
The boys running ahead.
You and dad in the ground.

And me walking
somewhere in between.

Life in Reverse

She left her shells
on the beach
as she went in.
Let the earth's own moisture
fill the crevices
of her soul.

The woman whose heart
waited eclipsed,
for a day to run
young again.

Waited in the bride's room
for the husband,
children
in her dream life.

She had written a poem
alone on the evening
of her junior prom,
encapsulated silence.

Words learned, scribbled
with pencil,
captioned a cut out picture.

When she was a child,
waiting to grow up.

Underneath

Take notes
if you need to,
while I tell you
how I learned to swim
inside a dark building.

Could not see the bottom
past the five foot level.
Cried all the way to lessons.

How I closed my eyes
while I swam the backstroke
to the edge of the black
and back.

Never became a good swimmer.
Fearing deep water,
not because I could slip
into it and sleep forever
rolling in its depths.

Because even now,
in the clearest lake,
my white legs moving
in a glint of sun,
an intrusion to those below
watching.

Visiting Ghosts and Ground

I drove three hours
to smell the wild daughters
of my aunt's flower garden.
Hear the running bubbles
of *Lowry water* creek.
Run into myself
around the corner,
red hair flying
on the wooden swing

There is a breeze up here.
Singing still a duet
with robins and sparrows.
A voice they called
to my uncle
as he drove nails to board,
put his sweat and a name
on this cabin door.

I follow the dirt path
behind the place,
still lined with white rocks,
guiding the way
on midnight runs
to the cranny.

The outlaw's woodshed door
squeaks open,
as if he might come out
with kindling
for a cold morning fire.

A dark bird circles my remembering
on my way to the creek.

I sit down on a rock,
stick both feet in
between the water skeeters.
*I'm not going to town
to find graves,*
I tell the bird.

There is hesitation
as I latch the shed door,
not unlike the pause
at the sealing of
my father's casket.

I walk past the window
without looking in,
leave my flowers
across the pinewood chair
on the porch.

Kindred Incantations

I tried a spell when I was ten.
A penny coined in my birth year,
the name of my admired
and my mother's perfume.

Sealed them in a plastic terrarium
from a cereal box
meant to sprout seeds.
I held it in my hands,
said some words, hid it away.

Secrets unknown to me then
of our grandmothers
who would add a drop
of menstrual blood
to their husband's morning coffee.
An incantation to keep them faithful.

Pennies in perfume.
Red circles in dark drink.

Canyon Calling

I stand on the last
crag of rocks,
darkness eating my fingers
as the mountain takes the sun.

I remove my shoes,
pay homage
to ancient feet,
those who looked across
this giant bowl before me.

None can speak an unholy word here,
on the brink of this place,
where surely
voices of the gone
still ring back and forth
without end.

They listen,
these voices,
for the right question.

I should yell out
with my best magic voice,
but as the sky draws her blanket
over me,
I wonder whose voice
will answer back.

Annie's Men

She liked to cut out
paper dolls,
keep them orderly
in a box.

When I was twelve,
with curtains closed
against the evening light,
she told the paper dolls
and me
about men.

About cheaters being born,
some people
some day,
getting their dues.

How there were
no new men,
only copies
of old ones.

Advised me not to give away
my insides,
or believe what lips
might say.

She knew what to do
with her men,
curtains closed
against the evening light.

But in the morning,
in the new,
they were never
where she had
left them.

A Love for Loneliness

They were hours
I've lost track of now.
Those you glimpse
in dreams
but lose in light
of morning.

Long days
on end
in the bluish hue.
Loneliness sat with me
awhile,
then laid with me
in bed.

I let him stay
longer each visit,
unafraid
and even accustomed
to the silence he brought
as a gift.

Like the cold
that curled around me
from my cracked window,
he wrapped around my grief
and lived beside me,
until we both
longed for days
when blood was warm.

Dreaming Herself Alive

She had hair the color of the sun
when it's too bright to look at.
Ex-husbands she prayed
she would not see in heaven.

Her life went by as a season.
Changing color like leaves,
drying up before their wonder
can be revealed.

Songs came to her in dreams.
She could play them upon waking,
in the dark.
Her fingers dribbling
up and down the piano keys.

Paintings on her walls,
mostly unfinished,
landscapes of places not visited.

She was an old woman
with a clock and a floor heater,
always keeping rhythm.
Reading the Bible, Frost, Dickinson.

From her blue chair,
she fed me words
that ran around my head
and down my spine.

She's a dreamer, people said.
But when the color left her eyes
along with the faces in her scrapbook,
it was all there still,
in her vivid
musical dark.

From a Stolen Child

There are notes baked with years,
a document from the courthouse,
binding her at three years old
to the white family
who bought her for a quilt.

The seller, who was not her mother,
had been pleased to get such a bargain
for a stolen child.
The quilt, the woman needed.
It would keep her warm,
wrap her in burial.

The wind carried a song
and they were kind to the child.
She was called their *Indian daughter,*
given more schooling
than the agreement required.

The dirt was the same color of red
she could barely remember.
The sun pulled up the mountain
to cover himself each night.
In this place of belonging and not,
she lived to be over thirty.

Her daughter would give birth
to my grandpa.
I would sit on his lap,
compare my red hair
to his black hair.

I tried to picture her
in her pioneer clothing at school.
In the notes, it says as a child
she loved to bake bread.
Though she was not allowed
to mix it,
or touch her family's food
with her little brown hands.

The Question

Desire in the eyes
of the boy,
hands on her waist
waiting permission.

Smiling like someone
just given
an unopened gift.

A rolled up Navy uniform
reveals her nickname
Bunny
sewn into his arm.

The photograph fits
in the book,
before my father.

*Would I still be
your little girl,* I ask,
if you had married him?

She winks at me.
The question floats
over us,
into the past.

I tilt the picture sideways,
away from the ending.
A fiery harbor,
a plane flying
too close to it
singed the sky black,
the boy who flew.

I take one more
guilty look at his face.
The man who could have
erased me.

Still your Child

The only peace I found
in your absence,
tiny bursts of memory.
Familiar gestures
which make me forever
your reflection.

Additional Acknowledgments

I was blessed with amazing parents, and know they are watching from above. I am indebted to many wonderful writers, whose work inspires me. A special thanks to my family, and those friends who stay by me, Katie, Rynell, Kim, and my sister Minna. Thanks to Marianne Goodell for the beautiful cover art. I appreciate the editors who have published my work, and Finishing Line Press for giving this manuscript a home.

Stacy W. Dixon is the author of two poetry chapbooks, *A Pebble Thrown in Water*, published by Tiger's Eye Press in 2010, and now *Visiting Ghosts and Ground*. Her work has been published in journals and anthologies, and has been nominated for a Pushcart Prize. She has been writing (in some form) since she was a child, and loves how the written word connects us through time and place. She is also a mom, and a lover of yoga, books, antiques, English roses, and all things inspiring. She lives in Utah with her three sons.

www.ingramcontent.com/pod-product-compliance
Lightning Source LLC
LaVergne TN
LVHW041518070426
835507LV00012B/1655